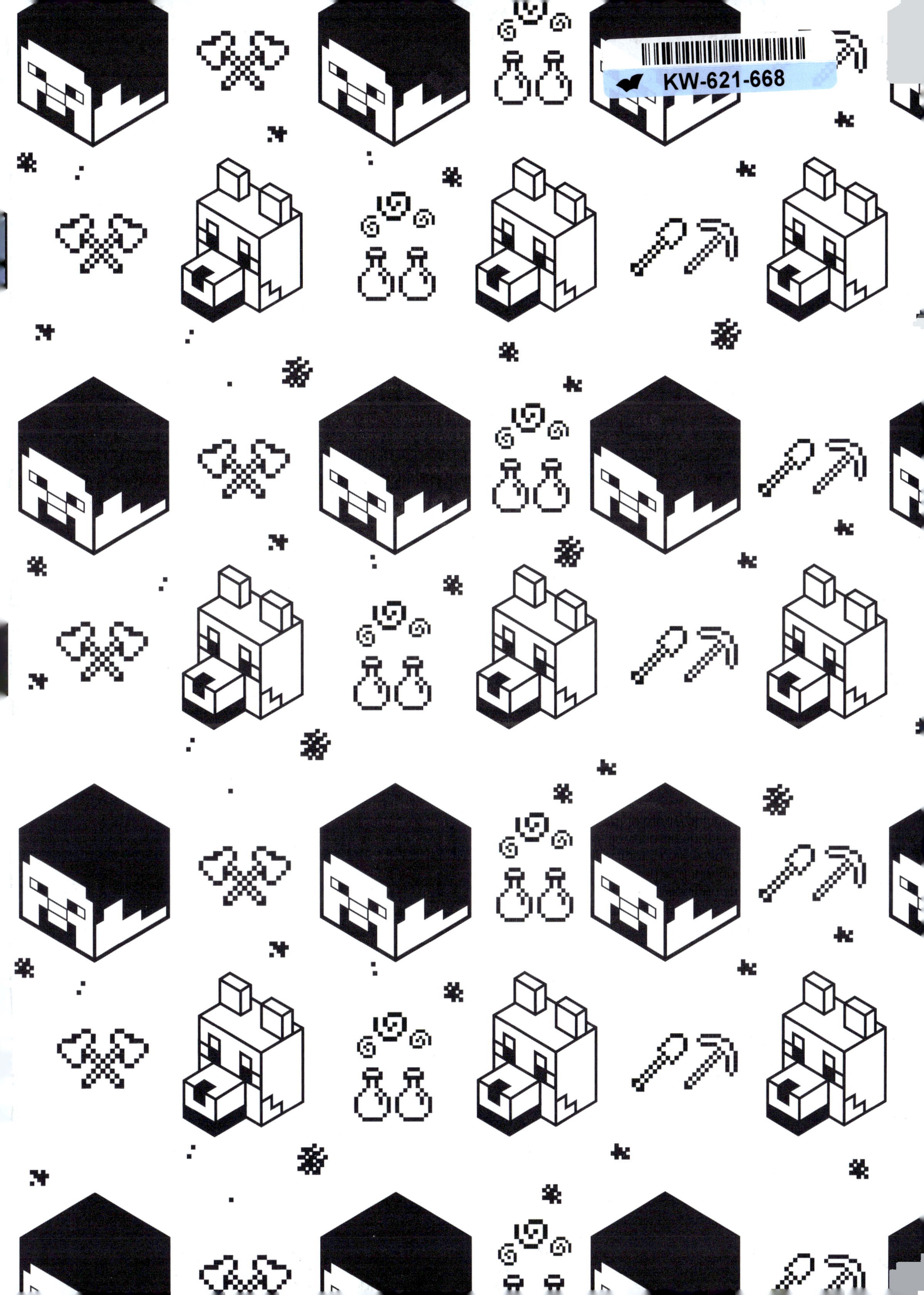

First published in Great Britain in 2025 by Farshore,
An imprint of HarperCollins*Publishers*
1 London Bridge Street, London SE1 9GF
www.farshore.co.uk

HarperCollins*Publishers*
Macken House, 39/40 Mayor Street Upper,
Dublin 1, D01 C9W8, Ireland

Special thanks to Sherin Kwan, Alex Wiltshire, Kelsey Ranallo, Lauren Marklund, Elin Roslund, Milo Bengtsson, Katie MacKay and Jill Benscoter.
Additional illustrations by George Lee
Additional images used under licence from Shutterstock.com

This book is an original creation by Farshore

ISBN 978 0 00 868220 0
1
Printed and bound in Romania

ONLINE SAFETY FOR YOUNGER FANS

Spending time online is great fun! Here are a few simple rules to help younger fans stay safe and keep the internet a great place to spend time:
- Never give out your real name – don't use it as your username.
- Never give out any of your personal details.
- Never tell anybody which school you go to or how old you are.
- Never tell anybody your password except a parent or a guardian.
- Be aware that you must be 13 or over to create an account on many sites. Always check the site policy and ask a parent or guardian for permission before registering.
- Always tell a parent or guardian if something is worrying you.

Stay safe online. Any website addresses listed in this book are correct at the time of going to print. However, Farshore is not responsible for content hosted by third parties. Please be aware that online content can be subject to change and websites can contain content that is unsuitable for children. We advise that all children are supervised when using the internet.

MIX
Paper | Supporting responsible forestry
FSC™ C007454
FSC www.fsc.org

This book contains FSC™ certified paper and other controlled sources to ensure responsible forest management.

For more information visit: www.harpercollins.co.uk/green

MINECRAFT

ANNUAL 2026

MOJANG STUDIOS

CONTENTS

KEY

- WORLD OF MINECRAFT
- CHALLENGE
- ACTIVITY
- A MINECRAFT MOVIE

HELLO!

It's been another exciting year in the blocky world of Minecraft and we're about to take a look back at some of the things that made it so special.

Over the past year, you've been busy exploring content from the Tricky Trials update and some epic game drops, including Armoured Paws, Bundles of Bravery and the Garden Awakens. Together, you've mined your way through more than 85 million biomes, tamed over 100 million wolves, placed over 300 BILLION blocks and helped us roll out the red carpet for *A Minecraft Movie*.

You've befriended eight new wolf variations, collected millions of armadillo scutes, and crafted armour to keep your trusty canine companions safe. You've mastered automated crafting, collected bundles of loot and built your dream bases – all without running out of inventory space!

When you wanted an extra challenge, you gave Hardcore mode a try, and many of you have even dared to venture into the eerie new pale garden biome, where you've followed the eyeblossoms and discovered something seriously creaky lurking beneath the hanging pale moss and pale oak trees ...

We'll get into that (and more!) in the pages of this Annual, so keep on reading! Whether you're building your first shelter, taming ALL the wolves, challenging a creaking to a staring contest, or taking on the trial chambers, there's something in here for everyone.

Let's go!

Lauren Marklund
MOJANG STUDIOS

A YEAR IN MINECRAFT

Wow, what a year it's been! So much has been happening in the world of Minecraft, including loads of fun updates, awesome collaborations and let's not forget *A Minecraft Movie*! So much has happened, so let's take another look at what's been going on, in case you've missed anything!

A MINECRAFT MOVIE

If you haven't seen this movie, you must have been hiding under a block! What are you waiting for? Starring Jason Momoa and Jack Black – it's a proper block-buster! Turn the page to find out more!

MINECRAFT EXPERIENCE

If you've been very lucky, you might have had the chance to immerse yourself in a Minecraft Experience. This is an interactive game experience that takes you on an adventure through Minecraft like no other!

MINECRAFT TETRIS®

Could two games ever be more perfect together? Squares meets blocks in this awesome collaboration that will have your eyes glued to the screen!

MINECRAFT BEATS

Let music shape your world! In celebration of Minecraft's 15th anniversary, Mojang teamed up with Beats by Dre to craft the special-edition Minecraft x Beats Solo 4 headphones. This collaboration celebrates the unstoppable creativity inside all of us.

CHOCOLATE PANDAS

We wouldn't blame you for being bamboozled into thinking these Minecraft pandas had leapt right out of the game. But can you believe that they were actually made out of chocolate?! Chef Amaury Guichon created this spectacular chocolate build to celebrate Minecraft's 15th birthday. Umm ... can we have a bite, please?

LUSH MINECRAFT

Just when you thought nothing could ever be more lush than a cave ... Minecraft and Lush came together to create a scent-sational range of bath bombs and soaps! Quick – where's the nearest bath?!

NEW PAINTINGS

A bunch of new paintings have been added to the game, created by artists Kristoffer Zetterstrand and Sarah Boeving. Have you checked them all out yet and chosen your favourite?

A MOVIE GUIDE

MEET THE HEROES!

A Minecraft Movie arrived this year and was a real block-buster! It's full of great fun, amazing mobs and awesome action. There's a good chance you've already watched the film, but in case you haven't, let's introduce you to some of the incredible characters, mobs and the portals you can expect to see on your screen!

THE PORTAL

When the unlikely duo of Henry and Garrett discover a mysterious portal hidden deep in a mine outside of town, they soon realise it is a pathway to a new realm full of adventure! What do they make of this strange, new Overworld?

STEVE

Steve isn't originally from the Overworld, but that hasn't stopped him from becoming a total legend there! Alongside his pet wolf, Dennis, he's a bona fide wizard of the cube!

DENNIS

Steve wouldn't have survived half as long if it weren't for his trusty wolf Dennis by his side.

NATALIE

Most of Natalie's time is spent looking after her little brother Henry, and hoping he doesn't get into any trouble! Between that and working in the potato chip factory, she doesn't have time for fun ... or does she?

BEE

Watch out for these adorable bees on your screen – they've generated a real *buzz*!

DAWN

In the real world, Dawn is always busy running her mobile petting zoo – so if anyone can help you survive in a world of new mobs, it's her. With all this new time to explore, will she discover some new skills to help her friends?

GARRETT

Garrett is a gaming superstar ... from a long time ago. These days, he has fallen on hard times and needs some luck. Will he find it in the Overworld, or will it be too much to handle?

HENRY

Henry is super smart and creative, but it often gets him in trouble. Luckily, when they all wind up in the Overworld, his skills are what they need to survive and try to save the day!

SHEEP

This is one of the rare, naturally spawned pink sheep. Finding one is *shear* luck and *ewe* can bet that the others were excited to see it!

BUILD CHALLENGE

STEVE'S CHICKEN SHACK

Feeling inspired by *A Minecraft Movie*? So are we! Let's add this plucky build to your favourite Overworld village! If lava is frying your chickens to a crisp (R.I.P. chickens), why not try this different approach to the im-peck-able movie build, using fire charges instead? With the flick of a lever, dinner will be ready in a flash!

DIFFICULTY: ★★★☆☆

30 mins

1

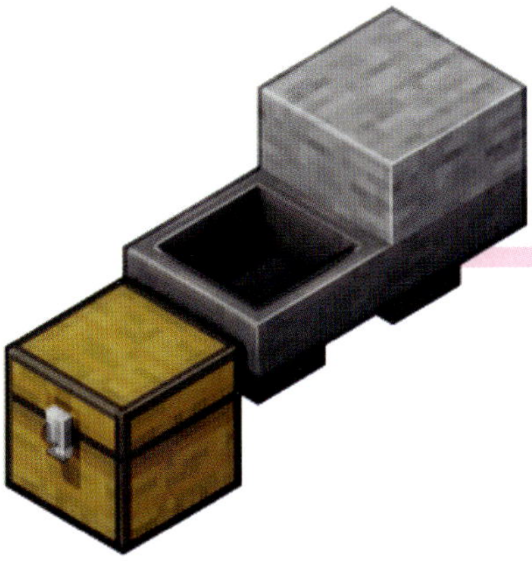

Start by placing a chest with 2 hoppers feeding into it from behind. On top of the back hopper, place a stone slab.

2

ROTATED 90°

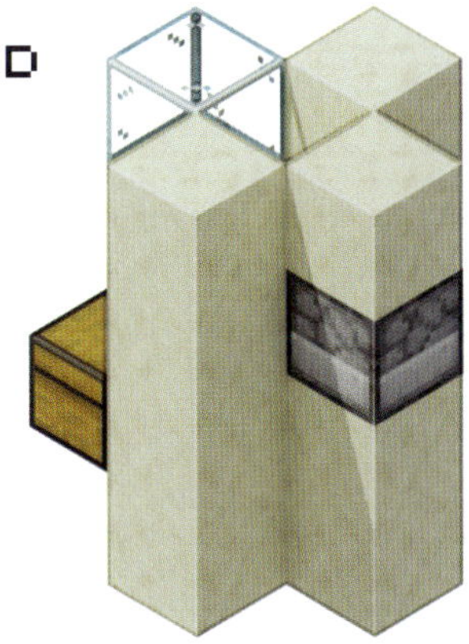

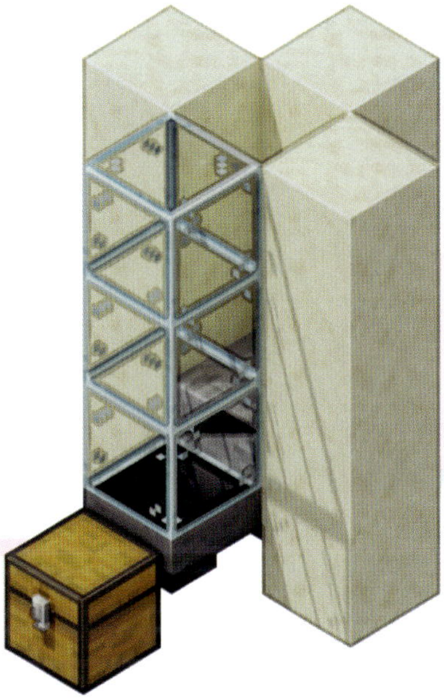

Behind the rear hopper, add 2 smooth sandstone blocks with a dispenser on top, pointed in the direction of the hoppers. Fill this with chicken spawn eggs. Add another smooth sandstone block on top, then build two more pillars on either side of the hopper, the same height. Place 3 glass blocks on top of your front hopper.

3

ROTATED 90°

On the back pillar, add one more smooth sandstone block, then stagger smooth sandstone slabs down the back of the contraption, down to a block above ground level, adding redstone dust to the top of each. A block above the hole between the sandstone, add a dispenser, face down and fill it with fire charges to blast your chickens.

4

Build a zigzag line with smooth sandstone that winds from the base of your staggered slabs to where the side of your building will begin. Use polished granite and upside-down oak stairs to build a side counter for your shack, then add a smooth sandstone block with a lever on it at the front. Connect it all with redstone dust and add a repeater to extend the redstone signal from the lever.

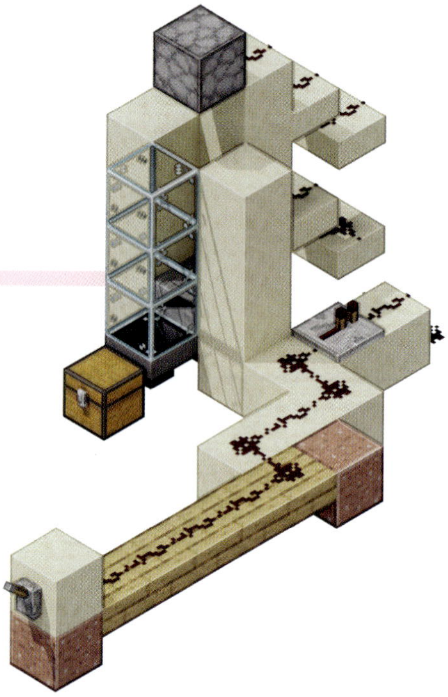

5

Now to build your shack! Using more polished granite and upside-down oak stairs to add countertops along the front and side. Then fill in the back wall with smooth sandstone.

6

Use more smooth sandstone to add pillars to the corners of your shack, then fill in the back walls. Join the spaces between the tops of your pillars with a mixture of red and white wool.

7

Add a ceiling to your shack using polished granite with upside-down stairs along the front and back. Use glass blocks to build triangular windows at the front and sides.

8

Use smooth red sandstone blocks and slabs to begin building the roof of your shack, following the shapes of your windows beneath.

9

Of course, no chicken shack would be complete without a chicken on top! Use white, black, yellow and red concrete to build your giant chicken, then fill in the rest of your roof with smooth red sandstone. Hen-sational!

A MOVIE GUIDE
HOSTILE THREATS!

LEARNING WITH PIGLINS

As if the Overworld didn't have enough baddies to keep you up at night, now its very existence is at risk from a ghastly invasion. The piglins want to find a pathway between their Nether realm and the Overworld, and they'll stop at nothing to get there. Let's take a look at these putrid piglins, as well as some familiar Overworld threats!

NETHER PORTAL

If the piglin armies are going to invade the Overworld, they'll first need a Nether portal to transport them there!

GENERAL CHUNGUS

Meet the ferocious first in command of Malgosha's armies. He uses his brute strength and tactical excellence to dominate and terrify the innocent creatures that stand in his path.

MALGOSHA

The fearsome leader of the piglin armies, Malgosha wants one thing and one thing only: to somehow gain access to the Overworld and exploit it!

PIGLINS

The foot soldiers of the Nether army do all of the dirty work. While they aren't the toughest, their numbers make them an overwhelming enemy.

GREAT HOG

It's clear which of these piglins is the Great Hog. This hulking mob is powerful enough to clear a whole group of enemies with one shot from his blaster!

ZOMBIE

They'll need to watch out for this rotten mob in the night! Though their movements are sluggish, they should never be underestimated.

SKELETON

The group of unlikely friends will need to watch out for these boney mobs in the Overworld – they might not have much muscle on them, but their aim can be deadly!

CREEPER

The unmistakable hiss of a creeper should never be ignored. As Garrett and the others soon find out, if you let this mob get too close, there are explosive concequences!

BUILD CHALLENGE

GHAST HOT AIR BALLOON

BUILDING WITH STEVE

What a ghastly sight! If you want to scare other players away from your base, these ghast hot air balloons will do just the trick – they look so real, even you might be scared to go home! And if you want to complete the picture, trap a couple of zombified piglins up there!

DIFFICULTY: ★★☆☆☆

20 mins

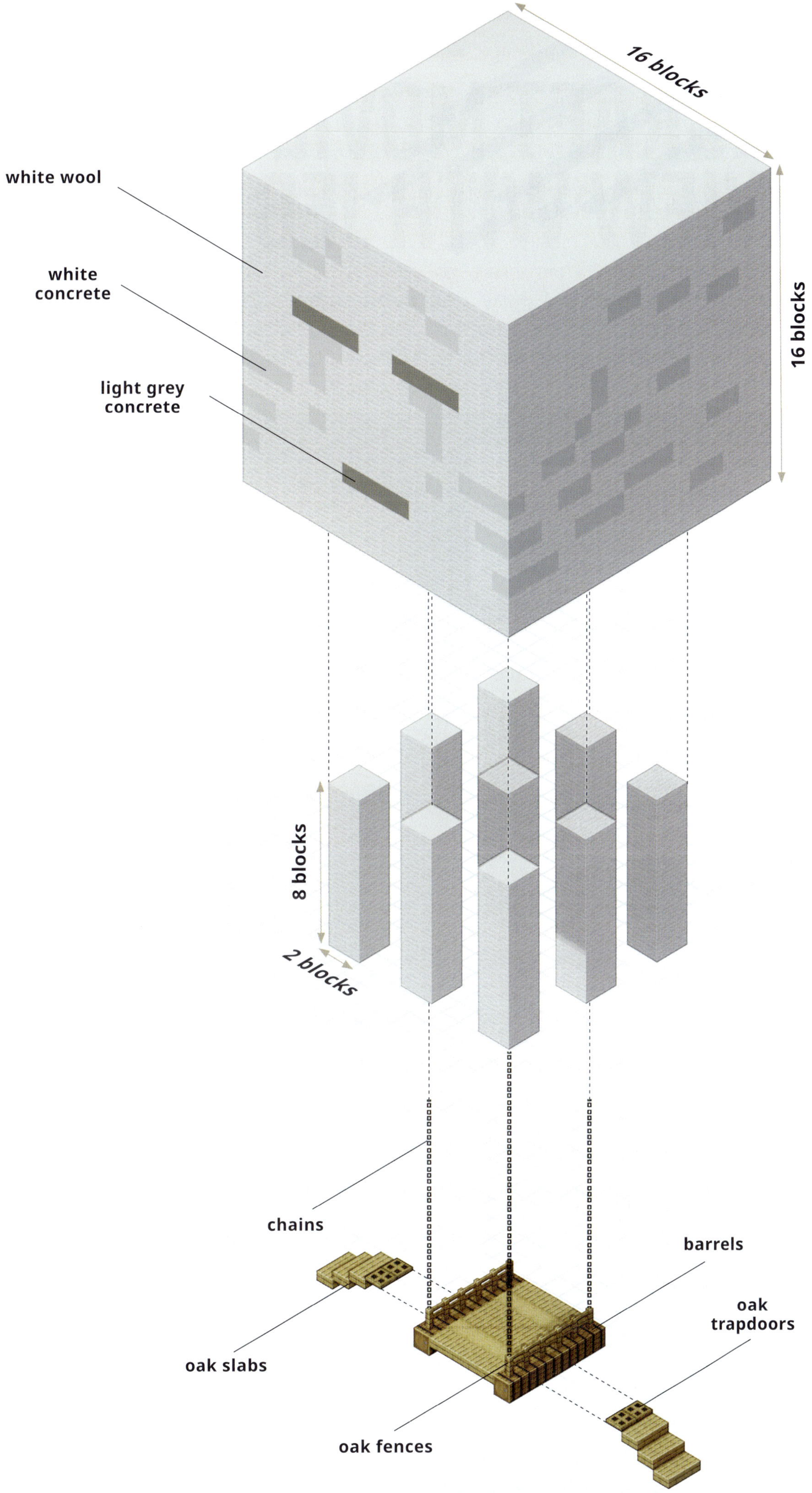

16 blocks
white wool
white concrete
light grey concrete
16 blocks
8 blocks
2 blocks
chains
barrels
oak trapdoors
oak slabs
oak fences

A MINECRAFT MOVIE INTERVIEW WITH JEB

Most of you will have already heard of Jens 'Jeb' Bergensten – Chief Creative Officer at Mojang. He is one of the original developers of the game and still works on it today. So of course he was heavily involved in bringing *A Minecraft Movie* to the screen. Let's ask him some questions about his time on set! Spoiler alert!

WHICH CHARACTER DO YOU IDENTIFY WITH MOST WITH AND WHY?

I guess it would be Steve, who wants to be creative and make cool things in Minecraft.

WHAT'S YOUR FAVOURITE STORY FROM BEHIND THE SCENES?

It was lovely to see how excited everyone was being part of *A Minecraft Movie*. There was such a good atmosphere and everyone really wanted it to become a great movie.

WHAT IS YOUR FAVOURITE MOMENT IN THE MOVIE?

My favourite moment is in the end when Malgosha, the evil piglin sorceress, tries to stab Steve with a hidden knife. It's funny because she is clearly lying and Steve isn't falling for it.

DID ANYTHING GO HILARIOUSLY WRONG?

I wouldn't say anything went wrong. There were more many happy little accidents, making everything more fun!

WHAT'S THE FUNNIEST THING THAT HAPPENED ON SET?

It was fun to see all the different variations of the script that was invented on the fly. Every scene had multiple takes with different dialogue to see which became the best or most funny.

MOVIE WORDSEARCH

Grab some popcorn and a pen, load up *A Minecraft Movie* and keep your eyes peeled for the clues you need to complete this epic wordsearch! Can you fill in the list of words from the movie below, then spot them in the wordsearch? You'll need to pay close attention to get them all!

B	J	E	R	G	Y	X	V	D	X	N	W	M	P	Q
L	S	B	T	R	A	R	N	A	T	A	L	I	E	P
D	G	E	N	H	Y	D	Y	W	Z	C	X	D	O	I
K	O	E	E	J	N	K	U	N	A	B	A	P	P	C
C	H	I	C	K	E	N	S	H	A	C	K	O	S	K
X	T	N	Y	R	N	E	A	R	G	R	S	R	A	A
U	A	A	N	T	V	L	T	H	M	G	X	T	B	N
B	E	J	C	E	Y	E	K	D	S	D	J	V	P	E
Q	R	S	T	B	B	G	L	Y	X	O	B	I	H	R
E	G	S	G	A	R	R	E	T	T	A	G	L	B	V
J	R	I	X	L	O	E	W	L	O	L	M	L	U	K
T	P	N	L	W	R	K	A	G	I	W	D	A	A	K
R	J	N	R	D	E	K	L	N	T	S	P	G	K	M
K	B	E	N	M	R	A	F	R	E	P	E	E	R	C
K	V	D	N	S	M	G	A	E	T	L	F	V	B	T
O	S	U	G	N	U	H	C	L	A	R	E	N	E	G

THINGS YOU'VE FOUND

- G______
- D_____
- S____
- H____
- N______
- D___
- M______ V______
- C______ S____
- C______ F___
- O________
- P_____
- M_______
- G______ C______
- G____ H__

Check your answers on page 70

KEEP ALL THE UPDATES COMING

Mojang have changed how they do game updates, opting to release them throughout the year, rather than focusing on just a major one. This means the updates are going to keep on coming in regular drops – yippee! Let's check out some of the latest things to be added to the game in case you've missed any!

WILDFLOWERS

Add a dash of colour to your landscapes with these blooming lovely new wildflowers.

BUSH

Finally, a bush to hide behind . . . if you crouch! Okay, so maybe you can't hide behind it. But doesn't it look nice and bushy?

MORE COWS

These new cows are udderly adorable! You'll now bump into both cold and warm cows across the Overworld – both of which are truly legen-dairy additions!

NEW PIGS

Weren't you just squealing with delight to find these two new friends hamming around on your screen? With both a cold and warm pig available to find, these mobs are sure to hog your attention!

FALLING LEAVES

Trees have been shaken up, and now their leaves drift down.

FIREFLY BUSHES

These bushes may look normal during the day, but at night they come alive with firefly particles!

BUNDLES

You can now craft a bundle from string and leather to store more items in your inventory. Each bundle can store up to 64 different items within it – including another bundle!

LEAF LITTER

With falling leaves, of course, comes leaf litter. You'll find these dead leaves scattered about on the ground of forests, roofed forests and wooded badlands.

EXTRA CHICKENS

There are two new plucky pals to find in the Overworld: the warm chicken and the cold chicken, depending on which biome you're in. Their eggs are even different colours – egg-cellent!

SHORT AND TALL DRY GRASS

Grass finally grows in dry biomes – well, kind of! It's a bit parched!

CACTUS FLOWER

Some cacti now grow flowers, adding some much-needed colour to the desert! You can use them for dye and breeding bees.

KEEP ALL THE UPDATES COMING

If you go into the pale garden at night, you're sure to get a creaky surprise. Let's check out some more updates!

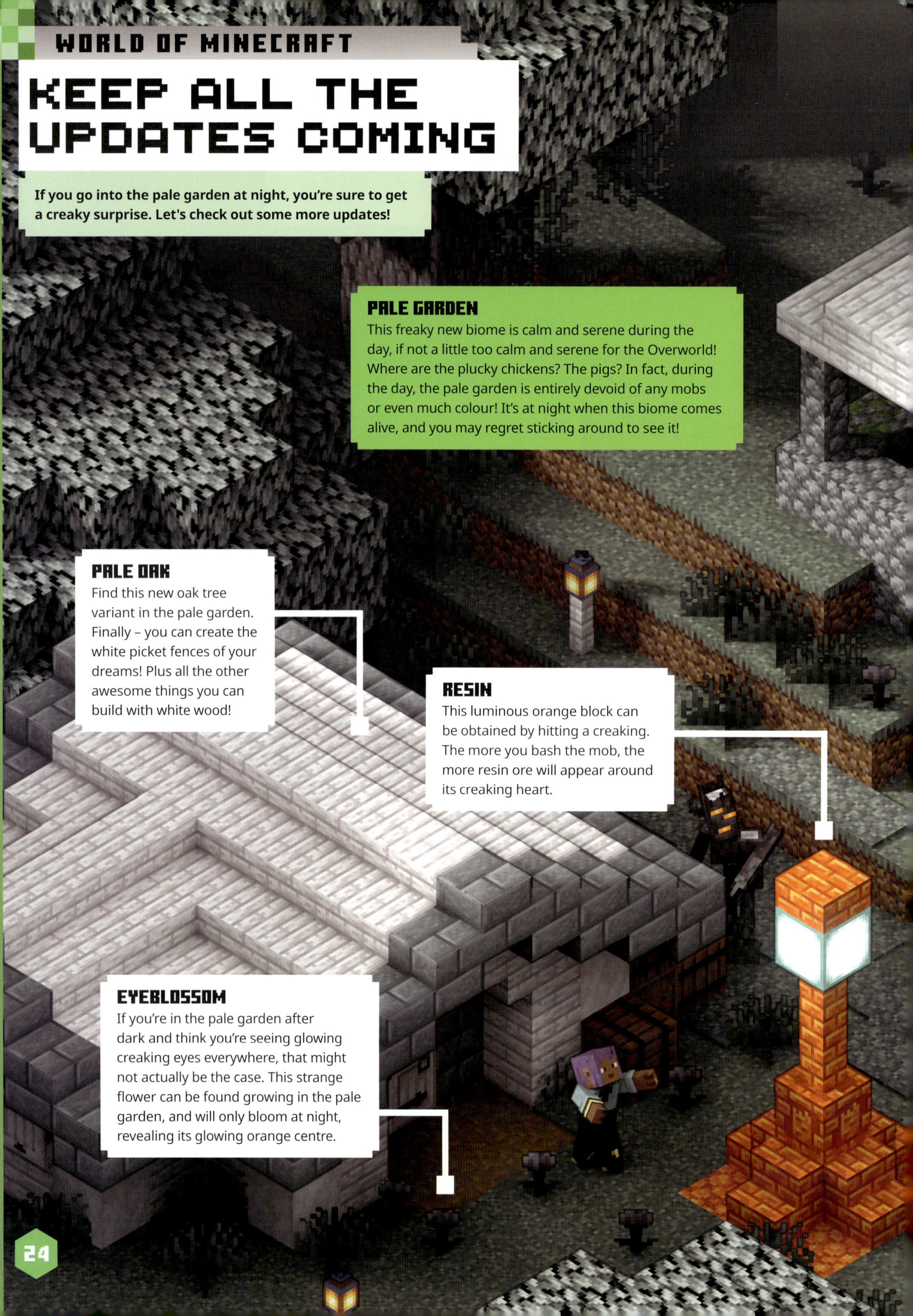

PALE GARDEN

This freaky new biome is calm and serene during the day, if not a little too calm and serene for the Overworld! Where are the plucky chickens? The pigs? In fact, during the day, the pale garden is entirely devoid of any mobs or even much colour! It's at night when this biome comes alive, and you may regret sticking around to see it!

PALE OAK

Find this new oak tree variant in the pale garden. Finally – you can create the white picket fences of your dreams! Plus all the other awesome things you can build with white wood!

RESIN

This luminous orange block can be obtained by hitting a creaking. The more you bash the mob, the more resin ore will appear around its creaking heart.

EYEBLOSSOM

If you're in the pale garden after dark and think you're seeing glowing creaking eyes everywhere, that might not actually be the case. This strange flower can be found growing in the pale garden, and will only bloom at night, revealing its glowing orange centre.

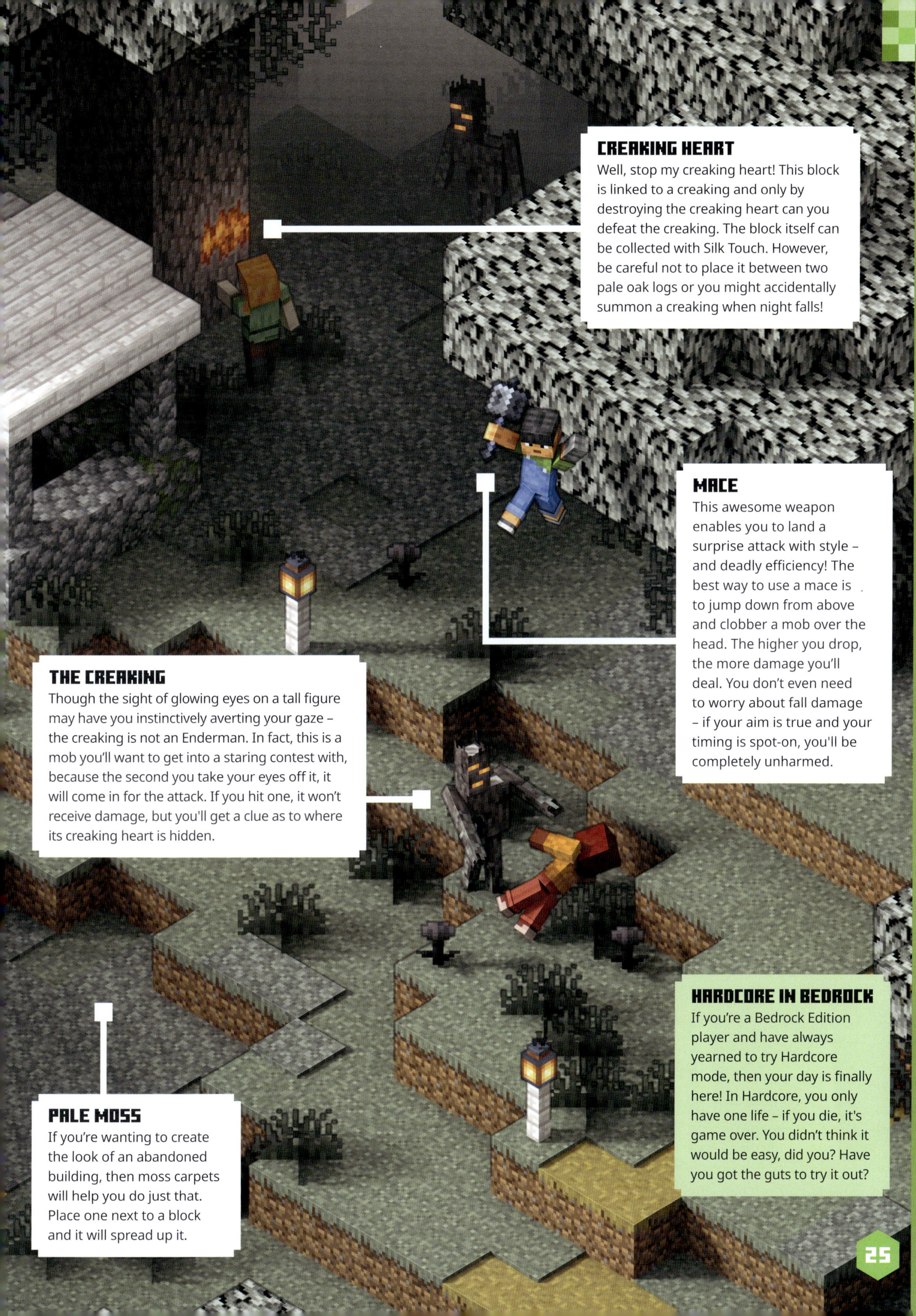

CREAKING HEART

Well, stop my creaking heart! This block is linked to a creaking and only by destroying the creaking heart can you defeat the creaking. The block itself can be collected with Silk Touch. However, be careful not to place it between two pale oak logs or you might accidentally summon a creaking when night falls!

MACE

This awesome weapon enables you to land a surprise attack with style – and deadly efficiency! The best way to use a mace is to jump down from above and clobber a mob over the head. The higher you drop, the more damage you'll deal. You don't even need to worry about fall damage – if your aim is true and your timing is spot-on, you'll be completely unharmed.

THE CREAKING

Though the sight of glowing eyes on a tall figure may have you instinctively averting your gaze – the creaking is not an Enderman. In fact, this is a mob you'll want to get into a staring contest with, because the second you take your eyes off it, it will come in for the attack. If you hit one, it won't receive damage, but you'll get a clue as to where its creaking heart is hidden.

PALE MOSS

If you're wanting to create the look of an abandoned building, then moss carpets will help you do just that. Place one next to a block and it will spread up it.

HARDCORE IN BEDROCK

If you're a Bedrock Edition player and have always yearned to try Hardcore mode, then your day is finally here! In Hardcore, you only have one life – if you die, it's game over. You didn't think it would be easy, did you? Have you got the guts to try it out?

BUILD CHALLENGE
CREAKING MANOR

BUILDING WITH SUNNY

This manor will leave you pale with fright! It may look abandoned, but you'd be mistaken to believe it's uninhabited. By day, it's a bleak sight to behold, with creaking floorboards, overgrown vines and cobwebs aplenty, but by night, the house takes on a terrifying twist. The creaking has claimed this house, and you are an uninvited visitor.

DIFFICULTY: ★★★★★

1 hour

1

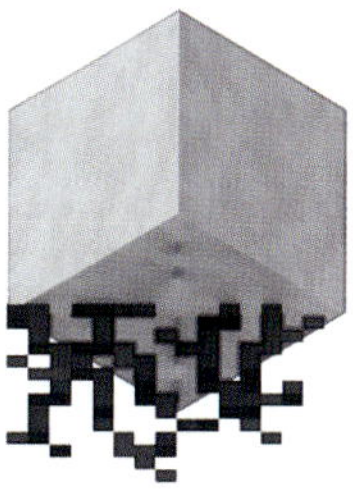

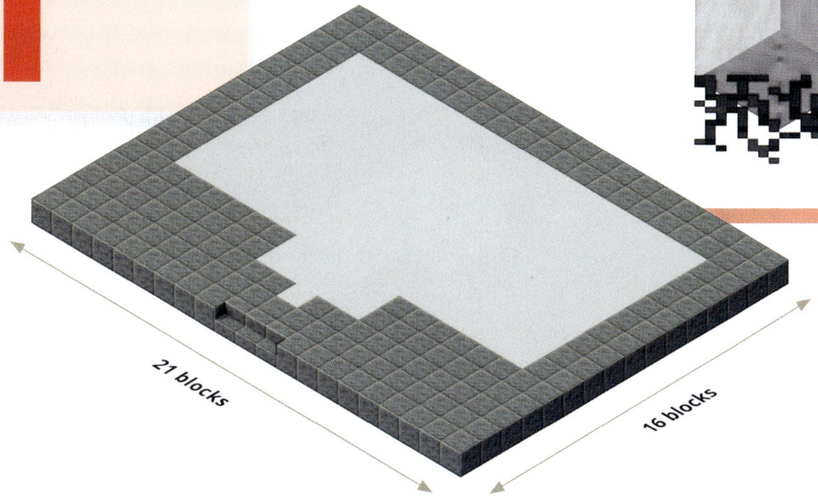

Dig a hole in the ground, at least 2 blocks deep and 17x9 blocks wide. Cover the hole with stripped pale oak wood with an additional 5x2 rectangle and a block at the front as shown. Go beneath the wood and place pale hanging moss beneath every block. This will make them creak eerily as if the manor is haunted. Add polished tuff around the edge of your foundation with 3 polished tuff stairs at the front.

2

Use pale oak planks to build 5-block-tall pillars around the corners of your stripped pale oak wood flooring. Place alternating blocks up the sides of the pillars on the four main corners.

3

Fill in the walls with pale oak wood, leaving spaces for windows with glass panes in them and a pale oak door at the front.

4

Build a porch above the front of the house with polished tuff blocks, using alternating upside-down polished tuff stairs around the edges. Prop it up with polished tuff walls and pale oak fences.

5

Add more polished tuff walls around the top of your porch with alternating iron bars. Then add polished blackstone buttons to the blocks around the outside.

6

Begin building the next floor by extending your pillars up another 5 blocks with more pale oak planks. Then fill in the floor with stripped pale oak wood, leaving a space for a grand staircase to come up.

7

Fill in your walls with pale oak wood, leaving spaces for windows and doorways, including a large 3x3 window at the front.

8

Add a large bay window at the front of the house, using glass blocks down the middle and glass panes on the sides. Add doors and window panes to the other spaces.

9

Build the final floor 7x7 wide, using pale oak planks for the corner pillars and the floor; pale oak wood for the walls; and a mixture of glass blocks and panes for the bay window to match the one beneath it.

10

Line the outsides of your upper two floors with upside-down polished tuff stairs, leaving the corners off.

11

Begin to build the roof above the centre floor using a layer of deepslate tile stairs, followed by a layer of deepslate tiles a block above and in.

12

Above your deepslate tiles, add a layer of deepslate tile stairs and fill in the rest of the roof with deepslate tiles.

13

Do the same again to build the upper floor's roof.

14

Around the edges of both roofs, build a layer of alternating polished tuff and polished tuff stairs. Then add polished tuff walls around the top, filling in the spaces between them with iron bars.

15

To make your manor look as though it's been abandoned for years, add plenty of cobwebs and pale moss carpets around it. Then, if you really want to make it haunted, build some pale oak pillars within your house, adding a creaking heart or two to them. You can even add them to the walls!

WOLVES 101

EXPERT GUIDE WITH ALEX

If you're a fan of wolves, then the Armoured Paws update would have had you howling with delight! There are now nine – yes, NINE – types of wolf to tame! Before you go on an epic quest to find them all (if you haven't already, we're sure you're about to), let's take a closer look at where to find them and what do to once you have!

BLACK
FOUND IN: Old growth pine taiga
PACK SIZE: 2–4

SNOWY
FOUND IN: Grove
PACK SIZE: 1

GOOD LUCK FINDING THIS ONE - IT'S A LONE WOLF!

CUSTOMISE

If you didn't think that was enough variation, you can now customise them with armour, too! Wolf armour is made by crafting six armadillo scutes together. You can leave your wolf's armour plain pink, or you can get creative and dye it. To do this in Bedrock, you'll need to first get a cauldron, then fill it with water and your chosen dye. You can even mix dyes in the cauldron to get different shades. There's an entire spectrum of colours to choose from!

If you change your mind and want to remove a wolf's armour, you can just shear it off.

You can also change the colour of your wolf's collar by using dye on it.

WOLVES 101

PERKS OF TAMING A WOLF

Not convinced that a wolf is for you? Here are some of the benefits of a tamed wolf.

GREAT COMPANY

You'll never feel alone in the Overworld again. Your trusty companion will follow you everywhere. So long as they're not sitting, they'll transport to your side if you get separated.

THEY'LL PROTECT YOU

Tame wolves will come to your aid and help defeat any mobs that are attacking you.

FRIENDLY

Once you've tamed a wolf, they'll no longer attack you, even if you accidentally hit them. But you wouldn't hit them, would you?

HELP HUNTING

If you attack a mob, your wolf will join in the action, finishing it off for you and leaving you the drops.

USE UP ROTTEN FLESH

Sure, wolves would love a juicy steak for dinner, but they'll also happily snack on rotten flesh, which will clear out some space in your inventory!

SUPER CUTE

Need we say more? Even their eyes get cuter when they're tamed! Adorable!

GRUB

Like you, your wolf will need feeding, as once it's tamed, it will no longer hunt nearby passive mobs independently. When your wolf is hungry, its tail will start to lower and it will start whining. So what's best to feed it? Check out the table below.

HOW TO CARE FOR YOUR TAMED WOLF

ARMOUR

We've already discovered just how cool armour can look, but what about the health benefits?

Your tamed wolf has a health of 40, which is already pretty great, but armour will protect it from most types of damage, adding the equivalent of 64 health points and making it nearly indestructible!

If you notice that your wolf's armour is getting a bit worn, don't worry about needing to craft it an entirely new set: you can just mend the armour it's wearing with more armadillo scutes.

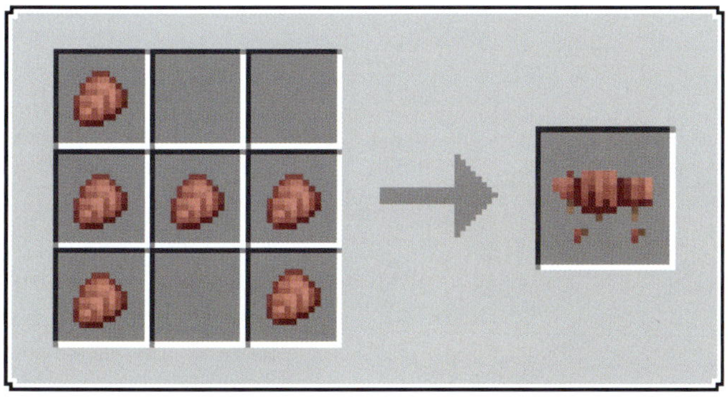

BOARD GAME MOBSPOTTERS

If you enjoy spotting mobs as much as we do, then you'll love this board game! Grab some mates or family members to play with, and roll the dice to move around the board, collecting the mobs as you go. The first one to collect all the mobs wins! Be warned, though, some of the mobs don't like you landing on them!

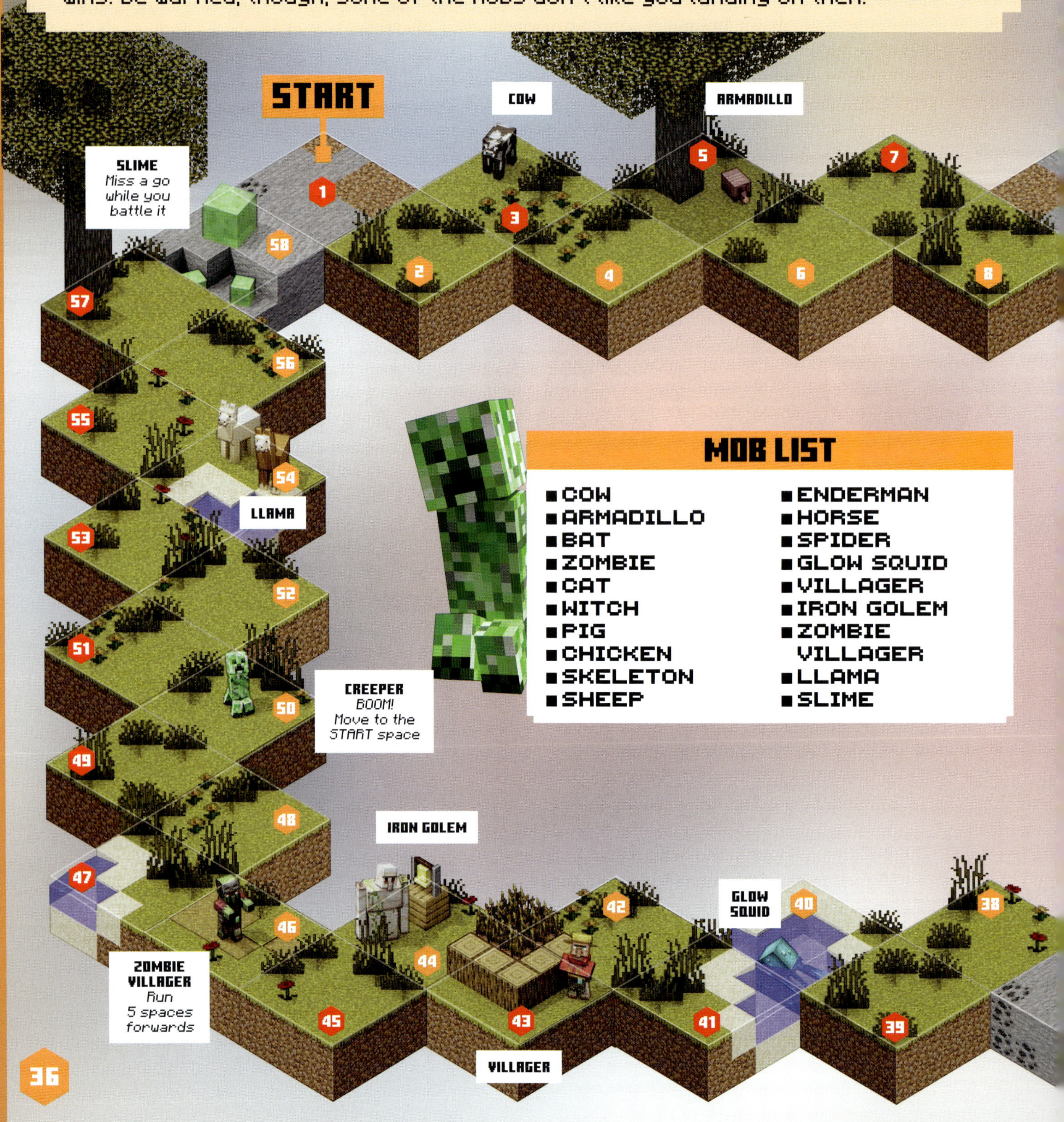

MOB LIST

- COW
- ARMADILLO
- BAT
- ZOMBIE
- CAT
- WITCH
- PIG
- CHICKEN
- SKELETON
- SHEEP
- ENDERMAN
- HORSE
- SPIDER
- GLOW SQUID
- VILLAGER
- IRON GOLEM
- ZOMBIE VILLAGER
- LLAMA
- SLIME

YOU WILL NEED:

- 2+ players
- 2 dice
- A counter each (you can make these with paper!)

RULES

1. Everyone grab a piece of paper each and write down all the mobs listed in the centre of the board game.
2. Roll a dice, moving your counter the number of spaces you roll.
3. If you land on a mob, tick that mob off on your list. Congrats – that's one less to collect!
4. If you land on a hostile mob, it might fight back. Complete the action on the space.
5. Keep on moving around the board in loops until someone has collected all the mobs.
6. The first person to tick off every mob wins!

SURVIVAL CHALLENGE
MANGROVE SWAMP

If you're a fan of water and frogs, you might consider settling down in a mangrove swamp. Though this biome may seem like an easy enough place to survive in, you'll likely find it more tricky than you first thought. With barely any passive mobs roaming about and no crops growing, finding food isn't going to be easy! Let's take a look at how to best survive in this biome.

1 CLEAR A SPACE

Mangrove swamps are densely packed, so if you're going to survive for long here, you'll want to make a clearing to build your base on. The added bonus of this is that you'll be collecting plenty of mangrove logs to craft tools with as you go!

2 CRAFT TOOLS

As you clear your space out, be sure to make a crafting table and craft some axes to help you finish the job. While you're at it, it's probably wise to craft yourself a sword or two, plus a pickaxe.

3 HIDE

Before night falls, you'll need to find a space to survive. If you have time, quickly craft some mangrove planks and build a tiny base. If not, climb up the vines of a mangrove tree and hide among the leaves until sunrise.

4 DEFEND YOURSELF

There's no use running in this biome: the foliage is too maze-like. Most of the usual hostile suspects spawn here, as well as a couple of swamp-specific mobs: bogged and slimes. Neither of which you want to be cornered by! Be sure to have a sword and shield at the ready and avoid the bogged's poisoned arrows!

5 FOOD TIME

There are only two sources of food here: tropical fish and honey. One is easy enough to catch if you dive into the water, the other will be impossible to eat without first getting a glass bottle. So unless you strumble across a witch who drops a glass bottle upon defeat, we hope you like fish!

6 BUILD A BASE

The building supplies aren't terribly varied in a mangrove biome, but that doesn't mean you can't make a spectacular base. There's lots you can do with mangrove trees: the wood inside is a gorgeous red colour and you can use shears to collect the leaves. Don't forget you can dig down, too. Beneath the layers of mud are the same blocks you can find under most other biomes. You may even find a trial chamber!

7 STRUCTURE AN ADVENTURE

With any luck, a ruined portal has spawned in your mangrove swamp. Among its loot could be enchanted golden armour and tools, and perhaps some useful items such as a flint and steel for you to light a fire to cook your tropical fish on. You may even find some alternative foods to munch on!

BUILD CHALLENGE
A BOGGED BASE

BUILDING WITH SUNNY

Are you being bugged by the bogged on your trip to a mangrove swamp? Why not build a base inspired by them? They might just be flattered enough to leave you alone ... or not! Don't forget to make sure your home is empty before you close the door behind you or you may wind up with some very rude uninvited guests!

DIFFICULTY: ★★★☆☆

35 mins

1

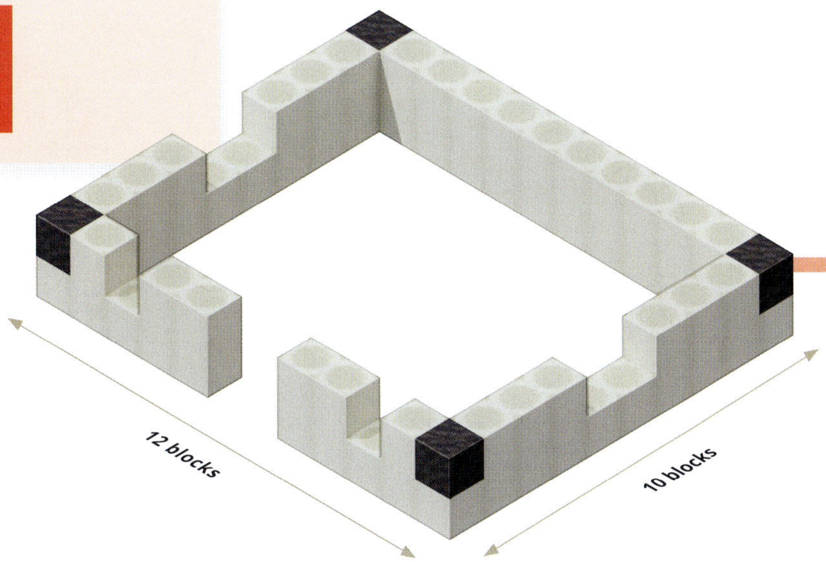

What are bogged made of? Bones, of course! Use bone blocks to create a 12 x 10 block structure, 2 blocks tall, leaving spaces for windows and a doorway. Add a mud block to each corner.

2

Add glass panes to each of the windows, and 2 mangrove doors in the doorway. Pop mangrove stairs on both sides of your side windows.

3

In case flattery isn't enough, let's camouflage your base! Use a mixture of mud and grass blocks on the sides to start making it look like a hill. Place another layer of bone blocks at the front and back of the base.

4

Continue to build up the sides of your base with grass and mud blocks, moving a block inwards to begin enclosing the roof. Add more bone blocks to the front and back of the base.

5

Add more mud and grass blocks around the top of your base, moving in a block on the sides.

6

Finish off your roof with mud and grass blocks.

7

Use a mixture of mangrove planks, stairs and fences to build frames around your front windows.

8

Use more mangrove planks and stairs to complete the circular porch, then add a bunch of lanterns dangling from chains for decoration.

9

Use a mixture of mushroom blocks to build two giant mushrooms, replicating the ones on a bogged's head.
Then finish off the build by further camouflaging it with short grass.

TAKE ON THE TRIAL CHAMBERS

EXPLORE WITH STEVE

By now, you've probably heard lots of talk of the trial chambers, and you may have even explored one or two. These underground chambers are full of dangerous challenges and bountiful loot, so whether you're still learning or a complete noob, let's get prepared – these pages might just save your life (in the game, of course).

HOW TO FIND A TRIAL CHAMBER

Firstly, check you're in the right dimension: if you're in the Nether or the End, then you'll have no luck finding one. In the Overworld? Great, let's get started! Trial chambers spawn just about anywhere in the Overworld, and are thankfully quite common. But that's where the luck ends with finding one: they're located deep underground, between Y -20 and 0. So how do you find one?

1 TRADE

If you're after a safer way to find one, then find a cartographer villager. You'll need a compass and a stack of paper and glass panes to level it up to journeyman. At this level, there's a chance they'll have a trial explorer map available to trade. Once you have the map, it will show you where a nearby trial chambers is. Tada!

2 DIG

Of course, you could just dig down anywhere and if you're mega lucky, you might stumble across one. But failing that, branch mining is your best bet for finding this structure. Get down to the right depth, then start branching out until you come across some tuff bricks or any copper blocks. If you find one of those, you've struck gold, or – in this case – copper!

3 CAVE

If you're a fan of exploring underground, then this option might be up your street/cave! Find a cave, steering clear of anywhere too mountainous – you'll want to avoid the deep dark as they're less likely to spawn near there. This method works best with a potion of Night Vision. Battle your way through caves until you find any tuff bricks along the walls.

WHY GO?

You might be thinking *Wow, that's a lot of effort to find a structure that's full of things that want to defeat me*, and you wouldn't be wrong. There will be a lot of mobs waiting to fight you, but isn't that part of the fun? Besides, if that wasn't enough to tempt you, then perhaps the loot will!

LOOT

Let's check out where to find loot in trial chambers!

CHESTS

Don't be disheartened if a lot of these are empty, though. They're there to help you with inventory management.

BARRELS

The items in these are fairly basic, but they sure come in handy!

DISPENSERS

If you don't accidentally trigger one of these and meet your doom, you might just find some handy items inside that may help in combat.

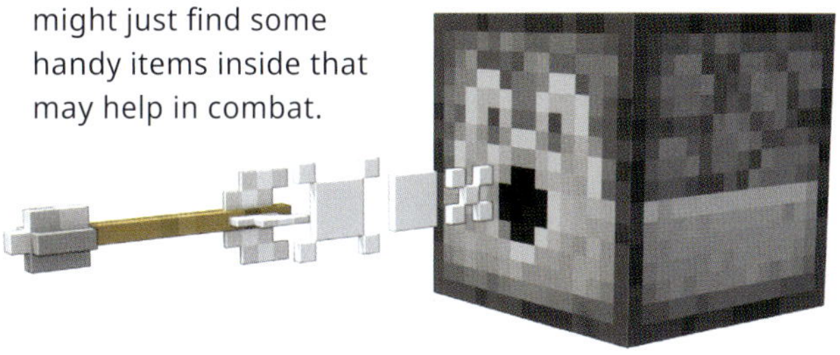

DECORATED POTS

There's some pretty good loot hiding in these, so don't be afraid to smash some pots!

TRIAL SPAWNERS

This loot comes at a price: you have to take down a bunch of hostile mobs first! But if you succeed in defeating them all, you may just be rewarded with a trial key.

VAULTS

This is where a trial key comes in handy. Only with one of those can you open the vaults, where you'll find some pretty awesome loot.

OMINOUS VAULTS

To crack into these vaults, you'll need to drink from an ominous bottle, which will summon mobs that are even more lethal than before. Defeat them all to get an ominous trial key to open these vaults.

TIPS FOR SURVIVAL

Now you know how to get there and what you'll find, let's take a look at some tips on how you can survive the trip!

WHAT TO PACK

Taking the right items in your inventory could be key to your success.

ENCHANTED TOOLS

Sure, your ordinary tools will be effective enough, but if you want to boss the trial chambers, consider enchanting your tools. Smite will allow you to defeat undead mobs with one swipe, while Sharpness will enable you to tackle the breeze with ease. Bane of Arthropods is your best bet for taking down spiders. And don't forget that you can enchant your bow, too!

AN AXE

This can be a regular axe. Though this might seem like an odd choice for a combat challenge, you'll need an axe to brighten up the space. Use one on a copper bulb and you'll remove the oxidation, making the light shine brighter.

A BED

Somewhere down in the trial chambers is a room FULL of beds. However, until you manage to find that safe haven, you might want to be extra safe and take a bed down with you. That way, if you are defeated, at least you won't spawn too far away.

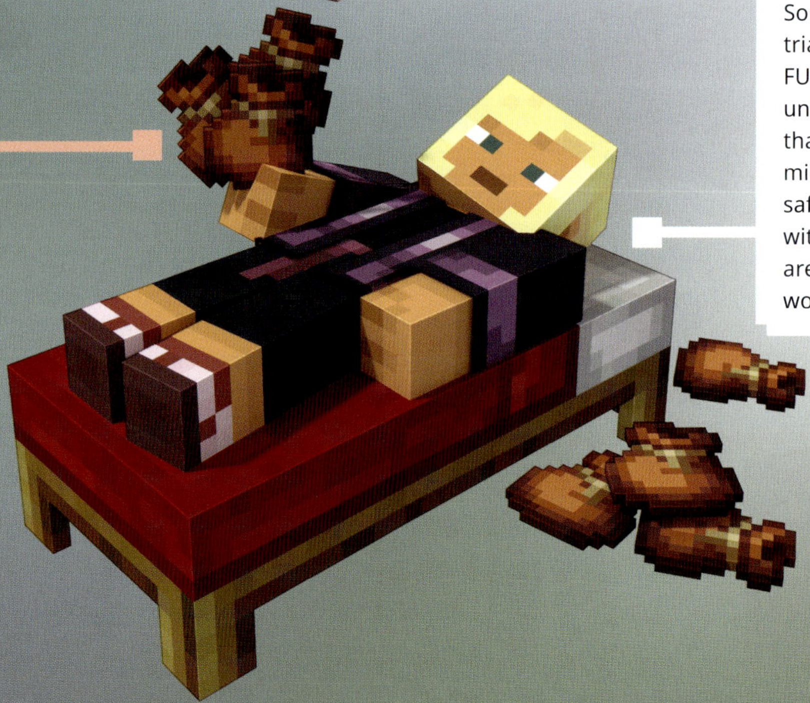

BUNDLES

While the chests dotted about the chambers are useful for storage, a bundle has the unique ability to store all its things within your inventory, extending the capacity of your inventory. What a bundle of joy!

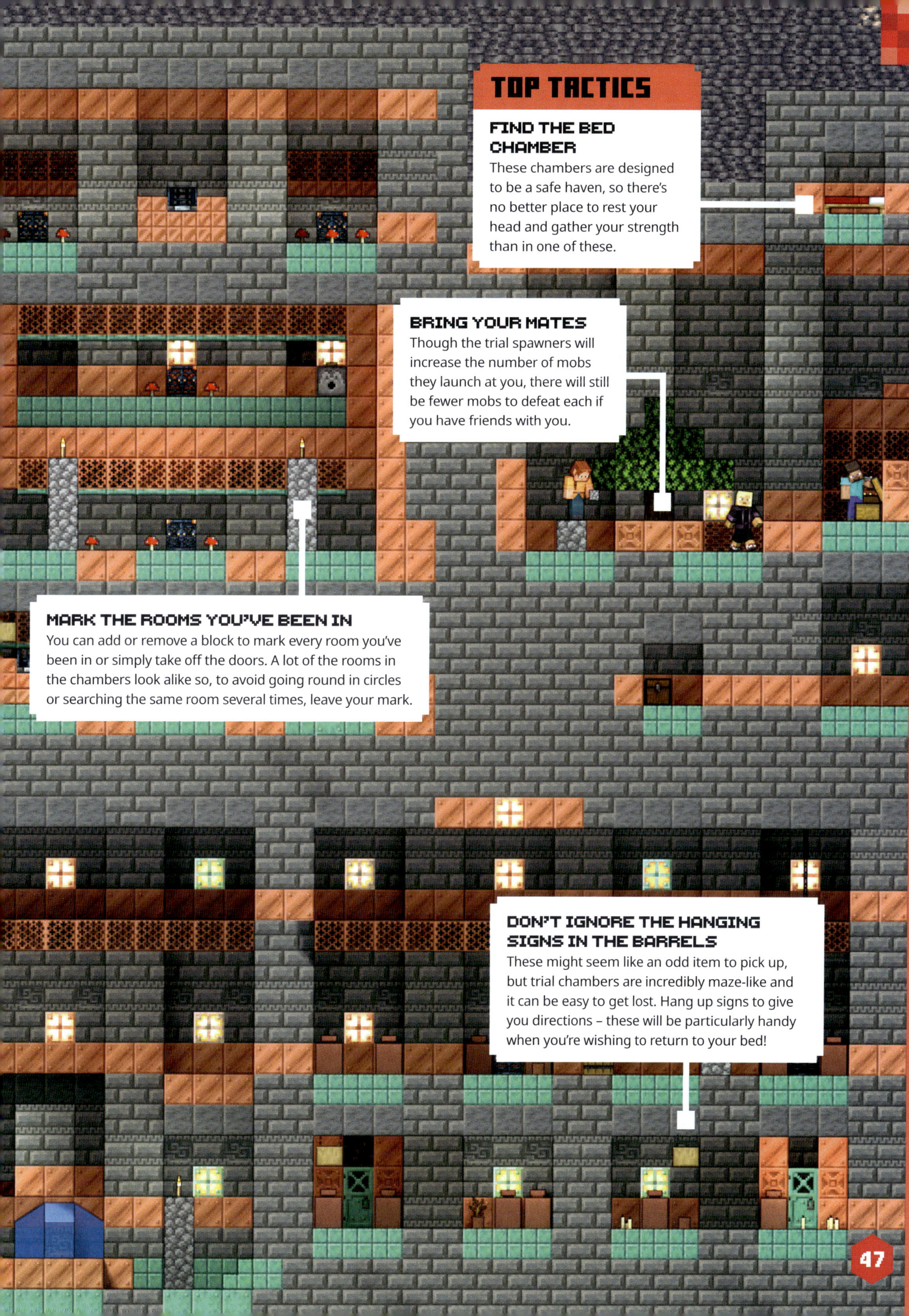

TOP TACTICS

FIND THE BED CHAMBER

These chambers are designed to be a safe haven, so there's no better place to rest your head and gather your strength than in one of these.

BRING YOUR MATES

Though the trial spawners will increase the number of mobs they launch at you, there will still be fewer mobs to defeat each if you have friends with you.

MARK THE ROOMS YOU'VE BEEN IN

You can add or remove a block to mark every room you've been in or simply take off the doors. A lot of the rooms in the chambers look alike so, to avoid going round in circles or searching the same room several times, leave your mark.

DON'T IGNORE THE HANGING SIGNS IN THE BARRELS

These might seem like an odd item to pick up, but trial chambers are incredibly maze-like and it can be easy to get lost. Hang up signs to give you directions – these will be particularly handy when you're wishing to return to your bed!

TRIAL SPAWNER QUIZ

Trial spawners have clues around them in the form of blocks. On the corners of each spawner are blocks that tell you which mob is going to spawn if you trigger them. This can give you vital time to prepare which weapons you're going to use. Can you correctly link the mobs to their trial spawner blocks?

Check your answers on page 70

ACTIVITY

WHICH MOB SPAWNED?

If you're not careful, you can trigger a trail spawner before you've had a chance to work out what you're up against and prepare for the fight. Can you follow the instructions below to colour in the grid and figure out which mob has just spawned behind you? With so many hostile mobs it could be, you'd better be quick!

	1	2	3	4	5	6	7	8	9	10
A										
B										
C										
D										
E										
F										
G										
H										

BLUE
2H, 3D, 3H, 4D, 4E, 4G, 4H, 5E, 5F, 5G, 5H, 6E, 6F, 6G, 6H, 7D, 7E, 7G, 7H, 8D, 8H, 9H

PURPLE
2B, 2C, 2D, 3B, 3C, 4B, 5D, 6D, 7C, 8A, 8C, 9A, 9C, 9D

LIGHT PURPLE
1E, 2A, 2F, 3A, 4A, 4C, 5A, 5B, 5C, 6A, 6B, 6C, 7A, 7B, 8B, 9B, 9F, 10E

NAVY
3G, 8G

YELLOW
2G, 9G

THE MOB YOU HAVE SPAWNED IS:

Check your answer on page 70

MINECRAFT MAZE
TRIAL CHAMBERS

You've battled your way through the trial chambers, surviving all manner of mobs and collecting all the loot. But wait. There's still one vault left unopened! Find your way back through the trial chambers, avoiding mobs and collecting the key to open the vault. Then it's time to skedaddle and get out of there before the mobs catch up!

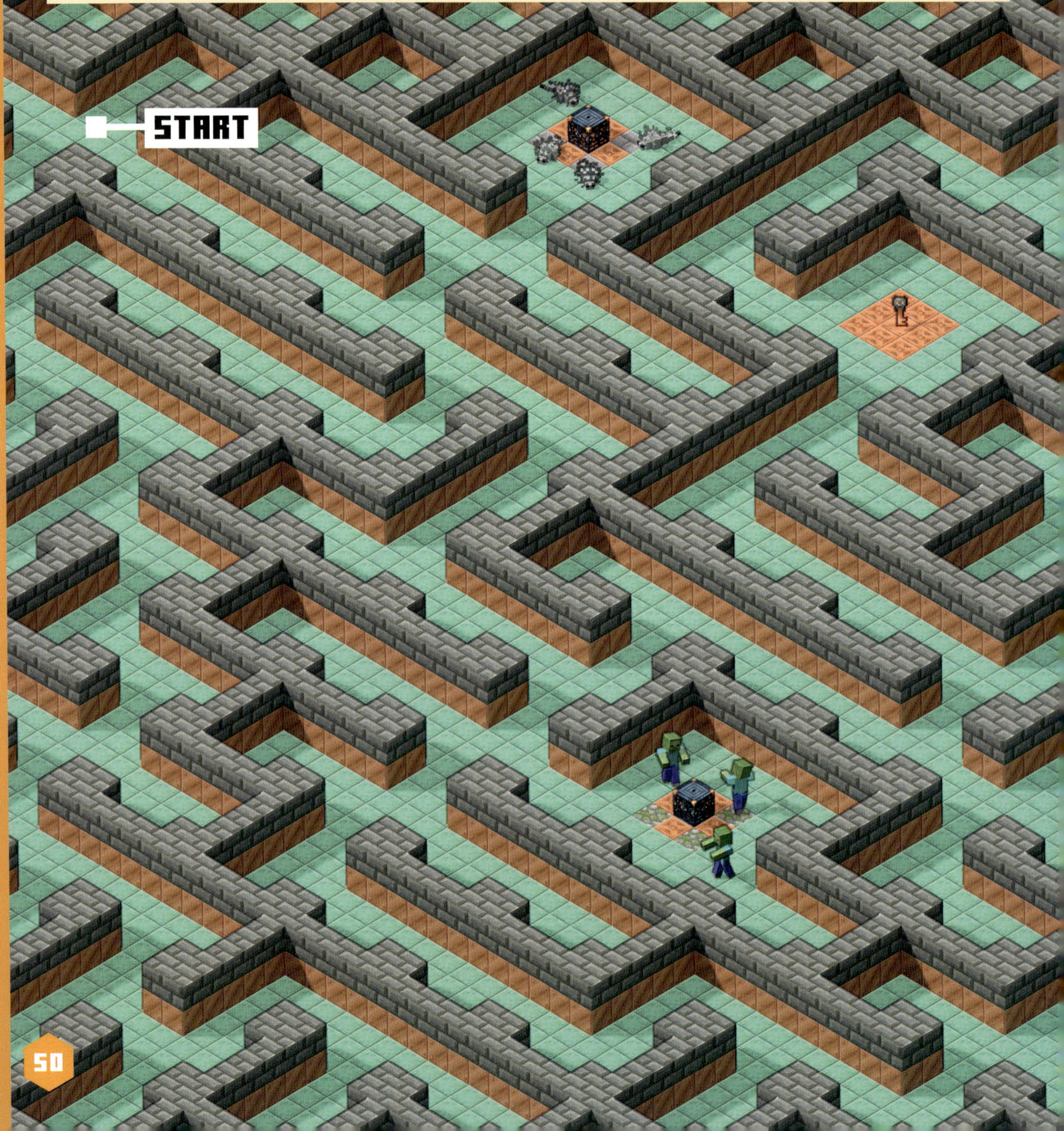

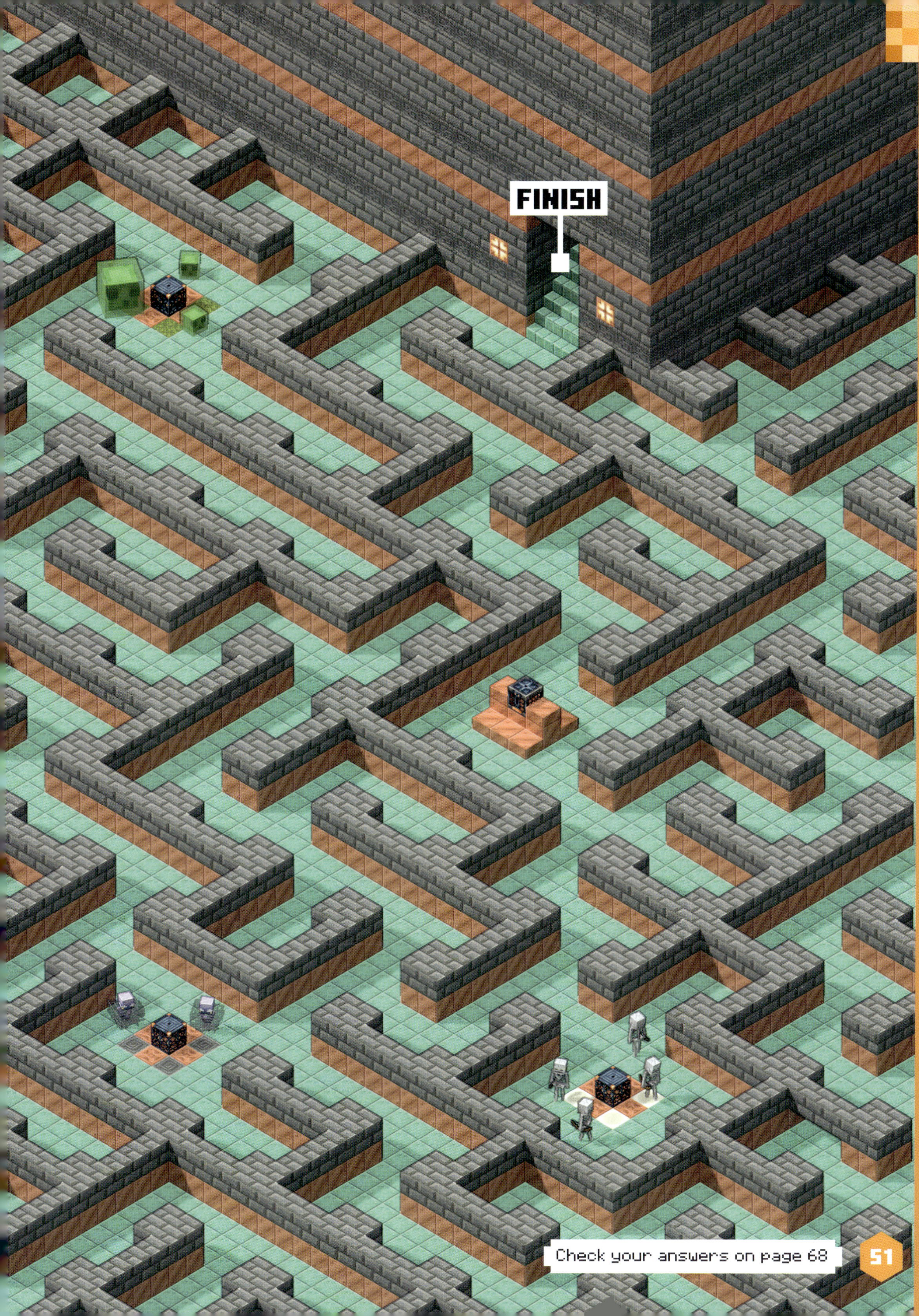

Check your answers on page 68

MARKETPLACE

Looking for a way to mix up your gameplay? Why not check out what's on Minecraft Marketplace? Whatever your vibe, you're sure to find a texture pack, mini game, adventure map or skin to make your game even more exciting. Love cute things? There are loads of adorable options!

TEXTURE PACKS

Change the look of your game with a texture pack!

REALISMCRAFT®

SPARK UNIVERSE

Want to see your game in a new light? This texture pack adds details and movement to blocks, and provides different lighting to completely transform your game.

PASTEL PARADISE

HEROPIXEL GAMES

If bright colours offend you and a muted palette is more your style, then you'll love this texture pack that turns your Overworld into a pastel paradise!

MASH-UP PACKS

Want a story and new textures to explore? Try a mash-up pack!

PIRATE MASHUP

HONEYFROST

Ahoy matey! AAARRR you ready for a wild adventure across the seven seas? Go on a swashbuckling adventure in this epic pirate mash-up pack, full of quests and treasure!

DRAGONS MASH-UP

EESCAL STUDIOS

Have you always wanted to ride the Ender Dragon but couldn't? Well here's your chance to be an epic dragon rider, taming and flying on the back of your very own dragon!

ADVENTURE MAPS

Embark on a new adventure with these immersive maps!

DR. SEUSS

SHALIQUINN'S SCHEMATICS

Take a deep dive into the stories of Dr. Seuss, going on an adventure through *The Cat in the Hat*, *The Lorax*, and *Oh, the Places You'll Go*! Which one's your favourite?

HORROR: THE ESCAPE

SQUARE DREAMS

What do you mean you haven't played this adventure map yet? Oh, the horror! Don't worry, there's still time for you to explore the dark forest and make it out alive – or is there?

MINI GAMES

Looking for a fun new game to play within Minecraft? Try a mini game!

CANDY LAND

TEAM VOIDFEATHER

You're in for a sweet treat with this delicious mini game! This candy kingdom is full of fun activities to complete, from parkour to mazes and even a monster forest.

PARKOUR WARS 2

THE RAGE CRAFT ROOM

Grab your mates and battle it out parkour-style in this thrilling mini game where each jump will either see you cheering or plummeting down to the lava below! Good luck!

SKINS

Give your player characters a makeover with a new skin pack!

BLOOM

YEGGS

Unlock your flower power with this beautiful skin pack that allows you to add florals to your outfits. You've never looked more blooming beautiful!

GHOSTLY TEENAGERS

FINGERMAPS

What's more scary than teenagers? Ghostly teenagers, of course! Embrace the dark side with these gothic skins that are hauntingly awesome!

WHICH BIOME SHOULD YOU LIVE IN?

Have you ever wondered which biome you'd live in if you were a villager? No? Well, let's change that! Whether you're imagining yourself as one of our long-nosed friends or just trying to figure out where's best to build a base, this quiz is for you. Follow your answers to find your ideal biome!

Do you like the cold?

- A No way!
- B Let it snow!

Would you rather have an inventory full of food or of treasure?

- A Loot all the way!
- B Bring me cake!

Is the grass greener on the other side?

- A Always!
- B Nah, I like my grass.

Which colour is your favourite?

- A Cactus green.
- B Sunflower yellow.

Which structure would you rather explore?

- A A desert temple.
- B An igloo.

Which log colour would you rather build with?

- A Acacia orange.
- B Oak and spruce browns.

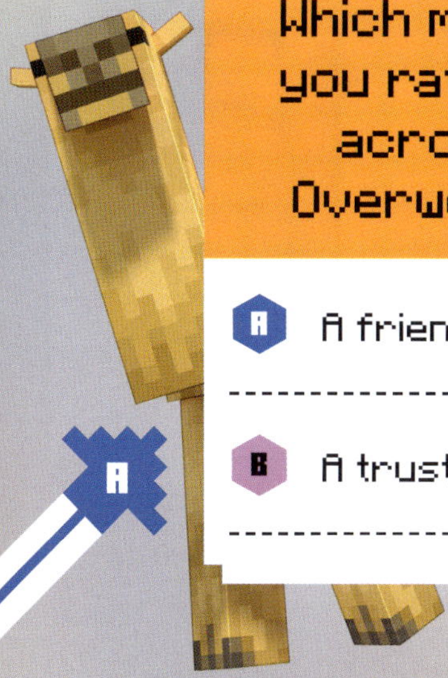

Which mob would you rather ride across the Overworld on?

- A — A friendly camel.
- B — A trusty horse.

Do you love food?

- A — Only when I'm hungry.
- B — I LIVE for food!

Which mob is cuter?

- A — An armadillo.
- B — A snow fox.

Which mob would you rather tame?

- A — A donkey to carry your stuff.
- B — A wolf to defend you.

DESERT

SAVANNA

SUNFLOWER PLAINS

SNOWY TAIGA

RARE MOB HUNT

EXPLORE WITH STEVE

We're all going on a mob hunt, we're not scared. (OK, maybe we are a little bit scared – screaming goats sound terrifying! What have they seen?!) If you're especially fond of mobs, then why not set out to find all of the rarest ones in the game? Perhaps you've even seen some already. Have you got what it takes to tick them all off?

SKELETON HORSEMAN

When lightning strikes during a thunderstorm, there's a chance that a skeleton trap horse will spawn. Get within 10 blocks of this and it will transform into a skeleton horseman, with three more nearby. Though the horse itself may be passive, you can bet the skeleton riding it isn't!

TOP TIP:

If you want to stop any of these rare mobs from despawning, name them using a name tag! Just be careful naming the charged creeper ...

INVISIBLE SPIDER

To spot this one, you'll need to set your difficulty to Hard. In this difficulty level, spiders can spawn with status effects, including invisibility. Keep your eyes peeled and you may just spot some red eyes staring back at you.

CHARGED CREEPER

This mob is best seen from afar! A creeper becomes charged when it's struck by lightning, which also makes its explosion range much bigger. RUN!

SPIDER JOCKEY

What could possibly be worse than an invisible spider? A spider with a skeleton riding it, of course!

PINK SHEEP

Now this isn't just any regular old sheep that you've sneakily dyed pink. No, this is a rare naturally spawned pink sheep. They can spawn anywhere there's sheep, so keep an eye out for this baa-rmy mob!

SWAMP AND JUNGLE VILLAGERS

These villagers won't spawn naturally, but they have their own outfits and enchanted books to offer! You just have to breed two villagers in one of these biomes to get them.

BROWN MOOSHROOM

To find a brown mooshroom, you could either try to breed red mooshrooms until you get one, or you can attempt something wild: you could get a red mooshroom struck by lightning, which will transform it. It might not thank you for it, though!

BROWN PANDA

Not only do pandas have different personalities, there's also a rare brown panda to be found in the jungle. Have your bamboo at the ready!

SCREAMING GOAT

Though it may look harmless, this mob will happily ram you off a mountain, given the chance. You'll need to turn your sound up for this one, as while it may look like a regular goat, it will sound very different!

BLUE AXOLOTL

You'll need to be incredibly determined to get one of these. Stock up on plenty of buckets of tropical fish as you'll be breeding axolotls for a while. There's only a tiny chance of breeding a blue one.

STORY QUEST: PICK YOUR WORDS

CREATE
WITH MAKENA

Are you ready to embark on an epic mini quest with us? On this page, all you need to do is choose your favourite words from the list – or, if you're feeling especially creative, you can write your own. So long as your words are similar to the ones provided, they should make sense. And, if not, then they'll be even funnier! Once you've chosen your words, fill them in on page 61.

1. Best, worst, awesome, smelly
____
2. Steve, Alex, Ari, Sunny
____
3. Groan, scream, fart, burp
____
4. Spin, turn, stumble, dance
____
5. Sound, belch, parp, yell
____
6. Screaming, deranged, angry, laughing
____
7. Tree, hill, bush, llama
____
8. Rams, tickles, prods, nudges
____
9. Horns, head, hooves, bottom
____
10. Mountain, peaks, slopes, frozen
____
11. Shove, tickle, poke, kerfuffle
____
12. Fall, topple, fly, trip
____
13. Cliff, block, tree, pig
____
14. Yell, squeal, sing, laugh
____
15. Flop, fall, fly, soar
____
16. Shouting, yodelling, gesturing, squeaking
____
17. Help, support, company, assistance
____
18. Far away, busy laughing, hungry, weak
____
19. Second, moment, tick, fart
____
20. Over, done for, safe, hilarious
____
21. Group, gaggle, swarm, herd
____
22. Chickens, pigs, cows, bees
____
23. Break, soften, ruin, speed up
____
24. Close, awesome, stupid, ridiculous
____
25. Safe, never going, eager, racing
____
26. Silly, epic, heroic, doomed
____
27. Cake, emeralds, axolotls, fun
____

CUT ALONG DOTTED LINE

CUT ALONG DOTTED LINE

STORY QUEST: COMPLETE THE STORY

Now for the really fun part! Fill in the words you selected for each number on page 58 to discover what story you've come up with! Will you be tickled by a goat's bottom or flop off a pig's back? If you enjoy this, you could even fill it out again on a separate piece of paper, or invent your own for someone else to complete.

You're out on an adventure with your 1____________ pal, 2____________, when you hear something 3____________ behind you. You 4____________ around to look for the source of the 5____________ when a 6____________ goat runs at you from behind a 7____________ and 8____________ you with its 9____________! You're in a 10____________ biome, so of course the 11____________ makes you 12____________ off a 13____________. You 14____________ as you 15____________ down, 16____________ at your mate for 17____________. But it's no use, they're too 18____________. But then, at the last 19____________ when you think all is 20____________, a 21____________ of brave 22____________ come to the rescue, and 23____________ your fall. Phew! That was 24____________! You're 25____________ to carry on your 26____________ adventure to find 27____________!

COMMUNITY CREATIONS

If you're ever looking for inspiration for what to build next, look no further than the incredible Minecraft community. People all over the world regularly share their amazing creations online for fans to feast their eyes on, and here are just a few to inspire your next build!

Copyright © @RobellaRose

COPPER HOUSE

BY ROBELLAROSE

'New updates bring new builds! This cosy starter house, using the new copper blocks, is the perfect place to hang out after a long adventure with friends. Dip your feet in the pond to cool off and pick fresh wheat for baking bread.' We love how the various copper blocks have been blended seamlessly into the landscape of this build! How can you incorporate more copper into your builds?

CELESTRIA'S EMBRACE

BY TRIXYBLOX

'I wanted to push Minecraft building to its limits with this creation, creating a vast, majestic castle with a vibrant colour palette, inspired by a unique mixture of architecture from all across the world!' This build is as huge as it is beautiful! Why don't you try out a similar colour palette on your next epic build?

Copyright © TrixyBlox

WORLD'S TALLEST TOWER

BY JERACRAFT

'I set out to create a tower that feels like it's emerged straight from the depths of a fiery underworld. Building this was a challenge, but I wanted every detail – from the rivers of lava to the jagged cliffs – to make you feel like you're entering a realm of raw, untamed power. Standing at the base and looking up, it's easy to imagine the ancient secrets this tower holds. My goal was to build something both beautiful and intimidating.' Can't you just feel the atmosphere of this build? We're both awestruck and slightly terrified! Can you build a base that evokes similar feelings?

Copyright © JERACRAFT

Copyright © @bluenerdmc

HARDCORE ZOO

BY BLUENERDMC

'This was one of my toughest builds, built entirely in Hardcore Survival mode over a three-month period. It was also one of the most fun builds I have ever done, creating a huge zoo for over 30 animals in Minecraft. It features a massive octopus build, where the mouth is the entrance to an aquarium for all the underwater animals. Till today, this is my most popular build on YouTube and still the one I enjoyed building the most.' That is seriously impressive! How many mobs can you build a sanctuary for in Hardcore without being defeated?

CITY OF TOMORROW

BY DIDDIHD

'I wanted to build a complex futuristic city inside a tropical jungle environment. I tried to create a mix of a dystopian and highly developed futuristic city and a city overgrown by vegetation that is in harmony with nature. I used a lot of glowing blocks, such as sea lanterns, frog lanterns and End rods, to add the final details to the unique look of the futuristic buildings. Green and watered roofs, vines on the walls and leaves, as well as mossy areas between the buildings, emphasize the nature.' Wow! We could spend all day exploring this city! How can you blend nature into your next build?

Copyright © DIDDIHD

LOOTING AN ANCIENT CITY

Ancient cities are vast, dark and – quite frankly – a little terrifying! With sculk sensors and shriekers everywhere, detecting your vibrations and summoning wardens to chase you away, you'd be forgiven for thinking this structure doesn't exactly want you there. But don't let that put you off: the chests in these cities are full of some of the best loot in the game. So let's see how you might go about surviving the trip!

WHAT TO PACK?

■ POTION OF NIGHT VISION
Placing torches sends out vibrations that could alert nearby sculk sensors, so this potion is your best bet of seeing what you're doing down there. You'll want several of these.

■ A BED
Like any potentially perilous adventure, it's always best to take a bed. Ancient cities spawn down near bedrock, so it would be frustrating to be defeated and find yourself on the surface again.

■ THE RIGHT TOOLS
Be sure to pack a hoe for breaking sculk blocks, shears for collecting wool, a bow and arrows for distracting the warden and an axe for breaking chests. And don't forget a pickaxe!

■ BUNDLES
There's a lot of loot to gather in an ancient city. If you want to bring it all back with you, pack a few bundles to collect your things in. You can even place bundles within bundles to take more home!

■ ARMOUR
You know, just in case. If you're wise, you'll avoid combat with the warden at all costs, but in case avoidance isn't an option, armour will help! But leggings are especially useful for the next item.

■ AN ANVIL
This is the only place you can get a Swift Sneak enchanted book. Once you've found one, if you have enough experience, you can use the anvil to apply it to your leggings to speed up your sneaking abilities.

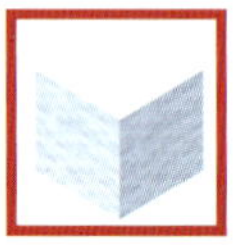

■ WOOL
And lots of it! Take at least two stacks, though you will find more down there. Wool can block the signals from sculk sensors and allows you to walk around silently, so long as you stick to the centre of the blocks.

■ TRAPDOORS AND OBSERVERS
Take several of these as backup for if the warden puts in an appearance. You can use them to make a nifty contraption to distract it while you sneak away.

FUN FACT

Ancient cities are the only place you'll find echo shards. Combine these with a compass, and you'll craft a recovery compass, which will point to the place where you last died. Now you can be reunited with all your stuff!

SNEAK
Crouch wherever you go. This may be slow without the Swift Sneak enchantment, but it will hide you from the sculk sensors.

THROW IT OFF
Snowballs can be thrown to fool the warden into thinking you're elsewhere. If you run out, they can be found in a chest within the ice box structure (search for ice blocks). Snowballs are a great distraction, but be sure to leave five seconds between each throw, or the warden will figure out it's being fooled.

TAKE DOWN THE SCULKS
Remove all sculk shriekers. Without these, there's nothing to summon the warden. Just sneak up on them, surround them on all sides with wool and break them with a hoe. The wool will stop them from sending signals to nearby shriekers.

DISTRACT THE WARDEN
If you accidentally summon the warden, then shoot an arrow in the opposite direction to you and use the brief distraction to place two observers facing each other with trap doors behind them both. These will create the perfect noisy distraction for the warden, so you can then sneak off and leave it behind. So long as you don't get within sniffing range or hit it, it won't follow you.

GET TO SAFETY
Another option for escape is to shoot an arrow to distract the warden and then very quickly build a pillar with wool, getting you high out of the warden's range. After a minute or so, the warden should despawn and you can climb back down safely.

BACK AWAY FROM THE FIGHT
Don't try to attack the warden. It has an immense 500 health points, so defeating it is unlikely. You're best off distracting it and staying away.

SPOT THE DIFFERENCE
SNOW FIGHT

PUZZLES WITH ARI

Brrr, it's freezing in the snowy plains – we hope you've packed some leather armour! Oh look, a snowball fight has broken out! Luckily, you have plenty of snowballs leftover from your ancient city adventure to join in with! Everything's moving so quickly, it's hard to take it all in. Can you spot the ten differences between the scenes below?

1 2 3 4 5 6 7 8 9 10

Check your answers on page 70

ANSWERS

21

B	J	E	R	G	Y	X	V	D	X	N	W	M	P	Q
L	S	B	T	R	A	R	N	A	T	A	L	I	E	P
D	G	E	N	H	Y	D	Y	W	Z	C	X	D	O	I
K	O	E	E	J	N	K	U	N	A	B	A	P	P	C
C	H	I	C	K	E	N	S	H	A	C	K	O	S	K
X	T	N	Y	R	N	E	A	R	G	R	S	R	A	A
U	A	A	N	T	V	L	T	H	M	G	X	T	B	N
B	E	J	C	E	Y	E	K	D	S	D	J	V	P	E
Q	R	S	T	B	B	G	L	Y	X	O	B	I	H	R
E	G	S	G	A	R	R	E	T	T	A	G	L	B	V
J	R	I	X	L	O	E	W	L	O	L	M	L	U	K
T	P	N	L	W	R	K	A	G	I	W	D	A	A	K
R	J	N	R	D	E	K	L	N	T	S	P	G	R	M
K	B	E	N	M	R	A	F	R	E	P	E	E	R	C
K	V	D	N	S	M	G	A	E	T	L	F	V	B	T
O	S	U	G	N	U	H	C	L	A	R	E	N	E	G

GARRETT
DENNIS
STEVE
HENRY
NATALIE
DAWN
MIDPORT VILLAGE

CHICKEN SHACK
CREEPER FARM
OVERWORLD
PIGLIN
MALGOSHA
GENERGAL CHUNGUS
GREAT HOG

48

HUSK C
BOGGED E
STRAY F
SKELETON D
H SPIDER
G BREEZE
A SLIME
B ZOMBIE

49

THE MOB THAT SPAWNED IS: A BREEZE!

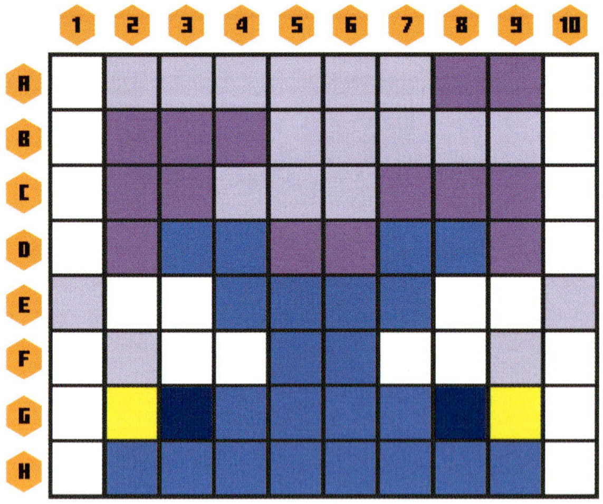

50-51

66-67

GOODBYE

That's a wrap on the *Minecraft Annual 2026*! We hope you've had as much fun as we have. Keep building, exploring and shaping your worlds, and we'll see you next year!

Lauren Marklund
Mojang Studios

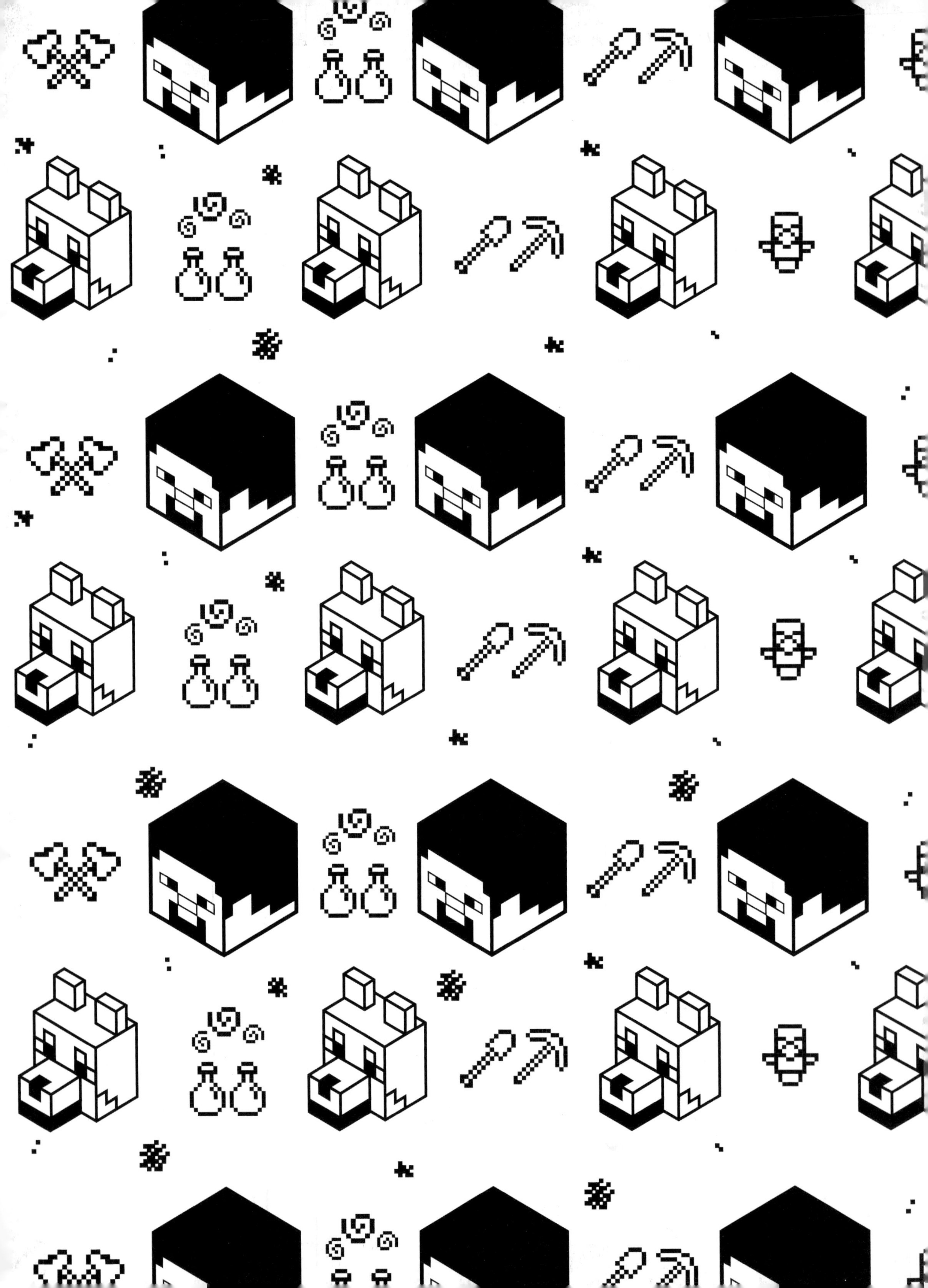